WITH ILLUSTRATIONS BY THE AUTHOR
JAMIE SMART

Dedicated To Me.
(Thanks!)

Looshkin
is a
DAVID FICKLING BOOK

First published in Great Britain in 2018 by
David Fickling Books,
31 Beaumont Street,
Oxford, OX1 2NP
www.davidficklingbooks.com

Text and Illustrations © Jamie Smart, 2018

978-1-78845-003-4

7 9 10 8

Papers used by David Fickling Books are from well-managed forests
and other responsible sources.

DAVID FICKLING BOOKS Reg. No. 8340307

A CIP catalogue record for this book is available from the British
Library.

Printed and bound in Great Britain by Sterling.

WARNING!

READING THIS BOOK MAY INDUCE THE FOLLOWING SIDE-EFFECTS: LAUGHING, A STRANGE SMELL OF GRAVY, GHOSTS COMING OUT OF YOUR EARS, HORSE NOISES, NOSE BALLOONS, A STARTLED PIG, ANOTHER STARTLED PIG, AN URGE TO CALL YOURSELF BERNARD, THE MOST HORRIFIC SQUELCHING NOISE EVER RECORDED, AND SNEEZING. HAIRBALLS, A STRANGE SMELL OF GRAVY, LOTS OF CRYING, MORE CRYING, SCARY CLOWNS,

ONCE UPON A TIME, A LITTER OF KITTENS WAS BORN. THEY WERE BEAUTIFUL AND CUTE AND EVERYONE WANTED TO OWN ONE OF THEM...

PETS

WELL, ALL EXCEPT ONE THEY HID OUT THE BACK...

ARE YOU SURE YOU WANT 'IM? 'E JUST AIN'T RIGHT.

STORE

THINGS GO...WRONG AROUND 'IM.

WELL, HE'S THE ONLY ONE LEFT.

WHAT'S HIS NAME?

BONK! ☆ SQUEAK! BONK!

LOOSHKIN

BUM!

AND SO BEGINS

OUR TALE OF...

FART!

...THE MADDEST CAT

IN THE WORLD.

BOSH!

FFRP!

PLEASE WELCOME THE NEW MEMBER OF OUR FAMILY! THIS IS LOOSHKIN!

A... A CAT?!

OH NO, NO, NO, **NO!** DARLING, I AM A **BRILLLLIANT SCIENTIST!** I CAN'T HAVE A **CAT** DISTURBING ME!

SOB!

I JUST WANT US TO BE MORE LIKE A NORMAL FAMILY. WE DON'T EVEN TALK ANYMORE!

WHEN I HAVE FINALLY PERFECTED MY **JET-PACK,** THEN WE CAN BE NORMAL.

FART!

©!!

©!! ☆ WELL, I THINK YOU'RE JUST IN TIME, CAT!

4

LOOSHKIN

THE CRAZY ADVENTURES OF... ...THE MADDEST CAT IN THE WORLD!

THIS EPISODE:

COLOUR IN
-WITH-
LOOSHKIN!

Colour in this PIG!!

oinkle!

Colour in this AEROPLANE!!

brmm!

Colour in my FACE!

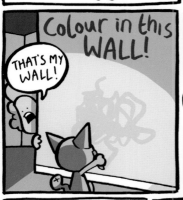

Colour in this WALL!

THAT'S MY WALL!

COLOUR IN GRANDPA!!

WAIT! STOP!

LOOSHKIN, YOU CAN'T GO AROUND COLOURING IN EVERYTHING YOU SEE!

SHAKE!

YES HE CAN!

THIS LIVING ROOM NEEDS A LICK OF PAINT! LOOSHKIN, THE WALLS ARE ALL YOURS!

SQUEAK-A!
SQUEAK-A!
SQUEAK!

SQUEAK-A!
SQUEAK!

HA! THEY SAW YOU COMING, DIDN'T THEY? THEY'VE TRICKED YOU INTO DOING THEIR HOUSEWORK!

10

THUMP! THUMP!
CREEEAKK!

SCREAM!

★ THUMP! THUMP!
CREEEAK! ★

SCREAM!

WHAT WERE THOSE NOISES?

THEY CAME... FROM THE ATTIC!

MIAOW?

WHAM! WHAM!

IS THIS ANOTHER SILLY JOKE, LOOSHKIN?

I THINK SOMEONE NEEDS TO GO UP AND CHECK.

IT'S YOUR ROOM. YOU DO IT.

ME? NO WAY!

YOU DO IT.

DING!

CREEEEEAK!!

NOOOO! WHY DOES IT HAVE TO BE MISTER BEAR?

SHAKE! SHAKE!

BAIT!

WOULD YOU STOP SHAKING ME AROUND, LOOSHKIN? I CAN'T SEE ANYTHING UP HERE. IT'S TOO...

...DARK.

CHOMP! CHOMP!

SHRIEK!

AUGH!

AARGH!!

SQUIRRELS!

YOU'RE MAKING FRIENDS!

THEY'RE ★ EATING MY FACE!

LOOSHKIN

THE CRAZY ADVENTURES OF... ...THE MADDEST CAT IN THE WORLD!

THIS EPISODE:

MOUSE HOUSE!

FART!

SCREAM! MICE!

HELLO.

THEY'RE **EVERYWHERE!** WHERE'S LOOSHKIN?

LOOSHKIN! WHAT...WHAT ARE YOU DOING?

I'M THE **MOUSE BUS!**

BOING! BOING!

YOU'RE SUPPOSED TO BE A **CAT.** YOU'RE SUPPOSED TO **CHASE** MICE.

RAWR!! THAT'S IT! NOW GO GET 'EM!

RAWR!

ABORT OPERATION STEAL-ALL-THE-CHEESE!

EVERYONE BACK TO BASE!

WE'LL BE SAFE HERE. THERE'S NO WAY HE COULD FIT...

I'M A **CAT! RAWR!**

☆**OOMF!**☆

DOOF!

OH.

A HAHAHAAA! THAT WAS **TERRIBLE!** AND I GOT IT ALL ON FILM!

WHAT A LOSER!

I'M GOING TO GO AND POST THIS ON THE INTERNET SO **EVERYONE** WILL SEE WHAT A STUPID CAT YOU ARE!

HA HA HAAAA!

I FEEL SICK.

MEANWHILE...

SIGH.

ANOTHER DAY OF EATING BISCUITS AND BROWSING THE INTERNET.

OH! WHAT'S THIS?

VIDEO

TRENDING

STUPID CAT BEING STUPID

5 MILLION VIEWS

BUY BUM CREAM

☐ LOL AMAZING
☐ OMG DID HE DIE?

CAT-LADY DATING ♥

HA HA HA! HOW SWEET! WHAT A FUNNY CAT THAT IS, HE DESERVES TO BE A STAR!

HANG ON!

IT'S THE CAT NEXT DOOR!

SANDRA

TELLY AWARD WINNER!

THIS IS MY CHANCE!

DING DONG!

HELLO, I'M YOUR NEIGHBOUR, **SANDRA ROTUND.** I USED TO PRESENT MY OWN DAYTIME TV SHOW, BUT MY CAREER ENDED AFTER I ATE TOO MANY SWEETS AND TRIED TO SHAVE MY STUDIO AUDIENCE.

I'VE BEEN WAITING ALL THIS TIME IN MY DRESSING GOWN UNTIL I COULD RETURN TO TV - AND YOUR **CAT** IS MY TICKET TO MID-MORNING STARDOM!

GLEE!

THEY'LL LET ME BACK ON TV IF I CAN GET A LOOSHKIN EXCLUSIVE!

THAT CAT IS VERY SPECIAL.

I HEAR THAT A LOT.

SO... WELCOME BACK TO **SANDRA,** MY BRAND NEW TV SHOW, STARRING YOUR HOST... **ME!**

sandra

AND WE'RE ABOUT TO MEET A REAL INTERNET CELEBRITY!

TV2

TV1

LOOSHKIN

THE CRAZY ADVENTURES OF... ...THE MADDEST CAT IN THE WORLD!

HAPPY BIRTHDAY, ME!!

HAPPY BIRTHDAY, ME!

AUGH! GET OUT!

SHOOF!

IS THIS A TRICK? IS THAT 'CAKE' JUST A BALLOON COVERED IN ICING, READY TO **EXPLODE**?

IT'S MY... BIRTHDAY.

YOU WON'T FOOL ME! NOT THIS TIME!

BIRTHDAY BIRTHDAY BIRTHDAY!

BIRTHDAY? CATS DON'T HAVE BIRTHDAYS.

WHAT DID YOU GET ME?

CATS. DON'T. HAVE. BIRTHDAYS.

WHY'S LOOSHKIN SO EXCITED?

PARTY PARTY PARTY!

DANCE DANCE DANCE

22

ALL ABOARD THE BIRTHDAY TRAIN!

ONK ONKK!

BIRTHDAY? IS IT MY BIRTHDAY?

HE THINKS IT'S **HIS** BIRTHDAY.

BUT LOOSHKIN, WE DON'T KNOW YOUR BIRTHDAY. WE DON'T KNOW WHEN YOU WERE **BORN**.

INSIDE LOOSHKIN'S HEAD...

DID WE BLOW UP ALL THESE BALLOONS FOR NOTHING?

NO. IT'S PROBABLY OUR BIRTHDAY.

WE. WILL. PARTY!

HANG ON, HOW DID WE GET OUT HERE?

BACK HOME...

WELL DONE, EVERYONE. PRETENDING WE'D FORGOTTEN LOOSHKIN'S BIRTHDAY SO WE COULD SET UP THIS SURPRISE **PARTY!**

AND HE LEFT HIS CAKE BEHIND, TOO!

NOW WE JUST WAIT FOR HIM TO SHOW UP...

HONK! HONK!

BIRTHDAY TRAIN!!

ONK ONKK!

HAPPY BIR

CHUFF! CHUFF! CHUFF! CHUFF! CHUFF!

HAPPY

HAPPY

BANG!

HA! I TOLD YOU!

SHOPPING LIST:
EGGS, BEANS, FISH FINGERS, CHUTNEY, MONSTER TRUCKS.

LOOSHKIN

THE CRAZY ADVENTURES OF... ...THE MADDEST CAT IN THE WORLD!

JEFF'S PHOTOCOPYING SERVICES. OUR PRICES ARE 'MAGIC'!

JEFF'S PHOTOCOPYING SERVICES. OUR PRICES ARE 'MAGIC'!

WHAT?

A WIZARD!

ME? OH, NO, THIS IS JUST A COSTUME.

A REAL LIFE WIZARD!!

NO, I WORK FOR THE PRINT SHOP, BUDDY. THIS IS JUST A COSTUME. SEE?

HNNRGG!

A REAL! LIFE! WIZARD!

JUST! A! COSTUME!

SQUEAK!

DO A MAGIC ON ME!

JUST GO AWAY! YOU'RE WEIRD!

JEFF'S PHOTOCOPYING SERVICES OUR PRICES ARE...

PLUH!

PLOOMF!

WHAT ON EARTH WAS THAT?

SALT! WIZARDS HATE SALT!

NO, THAT'S SLUGS! SLUGS HATE SALT!

THEN WHAT DO WIZARDS HATE?

WIZARDS HATE ANNOYING BLUE CATS WHO WON'T LEAVE THEM ALONE!!

CRACK
BOOM!

YOU GOT SO ANGRY, YOU MADE IT RAIN!

IT WAS GOING TO RAIN ANYWAY!

YOU ARE A WIZARD!

GALLOP! GALLOP!

YOU'RE A WIZARD! A WIZARD! WE CAN COMPETE IN WIZARD RACES AND EAT WIZARD SANDWICHES!

RRRGHH!!

FINE! HAVE SOME OF THIS!

ZZZAP!

HAPPY NOW?

YEAAAAA.

FOREWORD

By Professor Lionel F. Frumples
The World's Leading Expert On Cat Psychology

Cats! What are cats?

*Cats are **cats**.*

Zat is right, I'm an expert at cats.

I am brilliant at cats. BRILLIANT at zem.

I understand everything about cats. If you told me you were a cat,
I'd INSTANTLY know you were lying. I don't recognise your scent. Get
out of my office.

I wish I was a cat. As it is, I'm stuck being a stinky, filthy human
being. But I do still know a LOT about cats.

In fact, when I finish writing zis foreword, I shall be going to meet
another cat. His name is Looshkin, and his owners have asked me for
my expert cat advice.

I can tell you in advance,

I know exactly what I will be telling zem.

*Your cat is being a **cat**, you stupid humans.*

And they'll have to agree with me, because I'm so brilliant at cats.

Ok thx bye.

Yours sincerely,

I WAS WRONG!! ZAT FAMILY DON'T HAVE A CAT, ZEY HAVE A DEVIL! A DEVIL!

MRS TIDDLYWONK'S
REST HOME FOR PEOPLE
WHO THINK THEY'RE CATS

30

LOOSHKIN

THE CRAZY ADVENTURES OF...

...THE MADDEST CAT IN THE WORLD!

DING DONG!

DELIVERY!

AQUARIUM

HERE'S THE BABY SHARK YOU ORDERED.

BUT WE DIDN'T ORDER A BABY SH...

LOOSHKIN, DID YOU ORDER A SHARK?

IT'S **NOT** A SHARK!

IT'S AN OTTER!

YOU'D BETTER NOT BE RUNNING THROUGH MY HOUSE WITH A SHARK!

NOPE! OTTER!

WELL, OKAY THEN.

WHATEVER YOU THINK IT IS, WHAT ON EARTH ARE YOU PLANNING TO DO WITH IT?

ALL THE THINGS THAT OTTERS ARE KNOWN TO LOVE DOING!

DOMF!

22 19

DODGEMS!

THICK MILKSHAKES!

SCHUUUUUUP!

DRESSING UP LIKE SANTA CLAUS!

BUT IT'S JULY!

HEY! YOU CAN'T ARGUE WITH NATURE!

35

36

42

43

IMPORTANT MESSAGE:

It has co   ttention that readers   book

may be i   If you

think thi   ances

do not u   ents.

close all do   windows

and stockpile butter.

THIS WEEK FILMED IN GLORIOUS RASP BERRY -O- VISION!

LOOSHKIN

THE CRAZY ADVENTURES OF... ...THE MADDEST CAT IN THE WORLD!

THIS EPISODE:

THPTHBT THHHH HHHHH HHHHONK!

HOW RUDE.

THPTHBTHHH

HEY, LOOK AT LOOSHKIN! HE'S BEING FUNNY!

THPTHBTHH

WHAT IS IT, BOY? ARE YOU PRETENDING TO RIDE A MOTORBIKE?

HA HA! WHAT A SILLY CAT!

★ SLAM! ★

HA HA!

THPBTH HHH

WHAT'S WRONG WITH THAT CAT?

LOOSHKIN! MY NEMESIS! WE MEET AGAI...

WHERE ARE YOU GOING?

THPTHBTHH

WHAT'S GOING ON? HAVE YOU FINALLY LOST YOUR MIND?

STOP IT! YOU'RE SCARING ME!

HEE HEE! I THINK IT'S CUTE!

GASP!

WHO IS THAT?

47

LOOSHKIN

THE CRAZY ADVENTURES OF...

...THE MADDEST CAT IN THE WORLD!

KNOCK KNOCKITY KNOCK KNOCK!

AH, HELLO, OLD LADY, MY NAME IS **TERRY PICKLES, MP** AND I WAS WONDERING IF I COULD COUNT ON YOUR VOTE IN THE NEXT ELECTION?

GOODNESS, ARE YOU ALL RIGHT?

I'M AN OLD LADY!

WHAT NOISE DO OLD LADIES MAKE?

OH, YES.

I KNOW, BUT...UH...

BAROOOO

COME WITH ME, YOUNG MAN! YOU'RE JUST IN TIME!

IN TIME? IN TIME FOR WHAT?

...THE SÉANCE!

OBBBBBBBVIOUSLY.

DUH!

I, UH, I NEED TO GO HOME NOW. I'M SUDDENLY FEELING A LITTLE BIT GASSY.

THE SPIRITS!

HELLOOOOO, SPIRITS, ARE YOU IN THERE?

PARP ONCE FOR YES!

OOH! I THINK THE SPIRITS HAVE BEEN EATING EGG AND CRESS SANDWICHES!

NO LOOK, I REALLY DO HAVE TO GO.

NONSENSE! I'M ABOUT TO BE POSSESSED!

YOU ARE?

SCRAAAPE!

GNUUUUUUU UUUUUUU UUUU U U

WHAT ON EARTH WAS THAT?

A DEAD GNU. HE SAYS HE LOVES YOU AND IS VERY PROUD OF YOU.

I REALLY DON'T THINK...

SPLUTCH!

SHRIEK!

A POLTERGOOSE JUST STARTED THROWING TRIFLE!

THAT WAS YOU!

WE'D BETTER TURN OFF THE LIGHTS!

WHAT? WHY?

I CAN'T SEE ANYTHING!

WHAT'S THAT?

SOMETHING'S MOVING!

SHRIEK!

WHAT IS GOING ON?

WHO'S DOING THAT?

DOES ANYONE KNOW WHERE MY MAKE-UP BOX WENT? IT SEEMS TO HAVE GONE...

CLICK!

...MISSING.

DON'T WORRY ABOUT IT, LOOSHKIN.

WE WEREN'T VOTING FOR HIM ANYWAY.

JAMIE

53

LET'S PLAY... PIG OR FOSH?

PIG!

FISH!

PIG!

FISH!

FISH!

PISH!

FIG!

PIG!

MISTER TOMATO!

A FURIOUS BEAR!

MORLARK, THE TENTACLED LORD OF THE WAVES!

PFIGGLE!

 EEEEEEEE

 WHY CAN I HEAR THE CARPET SCREAMING?

 BEAR! THAT MUST BE BEAR! HE'S STILL ALIVE! I WAS ONLY TRYING TO GIVE HIM A NICE BIRTHDAY SURPRISE. ALL THIS IS JUST A BONUS.

 BUT HOW ARE WE SUPPOSED TO DRAG HIM BACK OUT FROM AN EVIL MAGICAL PORTAL IN THE FLOOR? WITH HAPPINESS AND LOVE!

 JUST KIDDING, I'LL GET HIM! FASHOO-OOM! SCAMPER!

 ✿THUMP!✿

 AM I IN? LOOSHKIN, THIS IS RIDICULOUS. MAYBE WE'VE LOST BEAR FOR GOOD...

 HELLO! ARE YOU HERE FOR THE PARTY? WELL, IT IS BEAR'S BIRTHDAY. IT IS! YOU'RE JUST IN TIME! PLOIP!

 COME INSIDE! COME IN! YAYYY! THIS IS GOING TO BE FUN!

 THERE HE IS! THERE'S BEAR! HUFF! PUFF! HELLO BEAR! HELLOOO!

 WHO'S YOUR NEW FRIEND? BRUM BRUM! HELP ME! HELPP MEE!

 WHY YOU RUNNING, BEAR? WHY? WHY? I'LL SHOW YOU WHY. BECAUSE IF I STOP...

PUT IT ON YOUR HEAD!

WHAT?

EVERY-THING!

LOOSHKIN

THE CRAZY ADVENTURES OF...

...THE MADDEST CAT IN THE WORLD!

THIS EPISODE:

YOU DID IT. YOU **FINALLY DID IT**

DING DONG!

PIG DELIVERY!

LOOSHKIN, HAVE YOU BEEN USING MY CREDIT CARD AGAIN?

DING DONG!

LOOK, WE DON'T NEED ANY MORE PIGS.

MISTER JOHNSON? I'M FROM THE COUNCIL.

WE'RE CONCERNED YOUR HOUSE MAY BE **UNSAFE** TO LIVE IN.

DUE TO A NUMBER OF INCIDENTS, INCLUDING A RAMPAGING CLOWN, A STEAM TRAIN, DANCING ELEPHANTS, PORTALS TO HELL AND **FREQUENT** TOILET EXPLOSIONS, YOUR HOUSE IS NOW STRUCTURALLY UNSOUND.

BUT...I'M AN **INVENTOR!** A **CRAFTSMAN!** EVERY TIME SOMETHING SMASHES THROUGH A WALL, I PATCH IT BACK UP AGAIN!

WELL, IT'S NOT ENOUGH. I'LL NEED TO CONDUCT A SURVEY.

GRR, THIS IS ALL **LOOSHKIN'S** FAULT!

WHERE IS HE ANYWAY?

TAP TAP TAP!

YOU ARE THE MOST BEAUTIFUL

CAT I HAVE EVERRRR SEEN!

THANK YOU MISTER BUNS, THAT IS VERY NICE OF YOU TO SAY.

LOOSHKIN, CAN YOU DO ANY BETTER?

I'M GOING TO EAT YOUR NOSE OFF!

LOOSHKIN

THE CRAZY ADVENTURES OF... ...THE MADDEST CAT IN THE WORLD!

THIS EPISODE:

Insert title here.
Make it something funny about pigs or monkeys or bottoms.
Frilly pants? Frilly pants are funny.

BRUM BRUM BRUMBRUM BRUM!

CHARLIE, STOP SINGING THE BRUM-BRUM SONG. YOU'RE SUPPOSED TO BE A PROFESSIONAL PILOT!

OH, YES, SORRY CAPTAIN!

I JUST GET SO EXCITED FLYING AEROPLANES!

ME TOO. HERE, I'VE MADE YOU A PICKLE SANDWICH.

WHAT THE... WHY IS THERE A SLEEPING CAT ON MY SEAT?

UMM...MAYBE HE HAD A BIG LUNCH?

WE'RE ON AN AEROPLANE, 30,000 FEET IN THE AIR! HOW DID A CAT GET IN THE COCKPIT?!

YAWWWN!

I WAS HAVING A DREAM ABOUT GUINEA PIGS.

GET HIM OUT! I'M ALLERGIC TO CAT HAIR!

UM...CAPTAIN?

HE APPEARS TO HAVE A SUITCASE WITH HIM.

AND IT APPEARS TO BE SCREAMING.

THUMP THUMP

MMF! MMF!

GAAAAAAAAA-AAASPPI REALLY NEED A WEE.

JUST GO IN THE SUITCASE. I DID.

YOU... WHAT? EW! EW!